Summary

of

SMARTER NOT HARDER:
(The bio-hacker's guide to getting the body and mind you want)

Michael L.Booth

TABLE OF CONTENT

Chapter 1

Dave Asprey, in his new book "Smarter not harder: The Biohacker's Guide to Getting the Body and Mind You Want." specializes in providing products and information to help people improve their physical and mental performance.

According to Asprey, biohacking is "the art and science of changing the environment around you and inside you so you have full control of your biology."

The book is separated into two sections, with the initial segment zeroing in on the body and the second part on the psyche.

Asprey discusses a variety of topics related to maximizing physical performance in the book's first section, such as nutrition, sleep, exercise, and supplements. Based on his own experience as well as scientific research, he offers recommendations that are supported by evidence for improving each of these areas.

In the second piece of the book, Asprey centers around techniques for working on mental execution, including care, contemplation, and cerebrum preparing. He provides advice on how to incorporate each of these practices into daily life and a comprehensive guide to each of them.

Asprey stresses the importance of individual experimentation and self-tracking throughout the book, encouraging readers to experiment with various biohacks and monitor their results to determine which one is most effective for them. When implementing any new biohacking strategies, he also emphasizes the significance of safety and working with a qualified healthcare professional.

The use of science and technology to improve one's mental and physical health is the topic of the book, which focuses on biohacking. According to Asprey, people can optimize their body and mind for peak performance by utilizing the most recent research in a variety of fields, including nutrition, exercise, and sleep.

The following are the four sections of the book: "Upgrade Your Relationships," "Upgrade Your Environment," "Upgrade Your Body," and "Upgrade Your Mind" The topics covered in each section range from exercise and diet to stress management and social connections.

Asprey provides advice for maximizing nutrition and discusses the significance of a healthy diet in the first section. He advocates a diet high in fat and low in carbohydrates because he thinks it can help people lose weight, have more energy, and think better. Additionally, he suggests supplementation and intermittent fasting for health improvement.

Asprey discusses the science of neuroplasticity and provides methods for enhancing mental health and cognitive function in the second section. He advocates biofeedback, meditation, and gratitude journals for stress reduction and improved focus.

The goal of the third section is to create a healthy and productive working environment. To create a healthier living environment, Asprey suggests implementing smart home devices and blue-light-blocking glasses. Additionally, he suggests spending time outdoors and getting plenty of sunlight.

Asprey emphasizes the significance of social connections and provides guidance for cultivating meaningful relationships in the concluding section. Empathy and active listening are two of his recommendations for strengthening relationships and improving communication.

Asprey backs up his claims throughout the book with research findings and personal stories. In addition, he provides readers with helpful hints and resources for putting the strategies he suggests into practice.

The book focuses on strategies and tactics to optimize body and mind performance with the intention of achieving greater success and fulfillment in life. It is aimed at anyone looking to improve their physical and mental wellbeing and offers a variety of strategies that can be customized to suit individual needs and lifestyles.

The authors argue that traditional strategies for achieving success, such as putting in more effort and working longer hours, are not sustainable and can result in burnout and a decline in well-being as a whole. All things being equal, they propose a biohacking approach, which includes utilizing science-supported methodologies to improve the body and psyche for max execution.

There are three main sections to the book: "The World," "The Body," and "The Mind" The authors discuss the significance of proper diet, exercise, adequate sleep, and stress management for achieving optimal physical health in the section titled "The Body." Additionally, they offer practical guidance on how to incorporate these practices into daily life.

The authors discuss the significance of mindset, motivation, and mental health for success in the section titled "The Mind." They offer methods for overcoming beliefs that hold us back and cultivating a growth mindset. In addition, they talk about how mental practices like meditation, mindfulness, and others can help people become more focused and productive.

The authors conclude with a discussion of the significance of community and social connections for success and well-being in "The World." They offer guidance on how to establish supportive relationships and discover life's meaning and purpose.

The authors provide case studies and real-world examples to support their arguments throughout the book. They also give readers practical exercises and steps to take to help them put the strategies in the book into practice.

The book is broken up into four sections. Whitten provides an overview of the fundamentals of biohacking, which involves utilizing science and technology to enhance human performance, in the first section. He explains the interconnectedness of the body's systems and how improving one can improve others.

Whitten focuses on the importance of sleep to overall health and performance in the second section. He offers practical advice for altering one's sleeping routine and discusses the significance of quality, quantity, and timing of one's sleep.

Nutrition and exercise are the topics covered in the book's third section. In order to achieve specific objectives, such as weight loss, muscle gain, or enhanced athletic performance, Whitten explains how to make the most of diet and exercise. He likewise gives data on enhancements and execution improving medications.

Chapter 2

The book's final section is devoted to mental performance and mindset. Whitten provides practical methods for enhancing mental focus and resilience as well as an explanation of the scientific foundations of habits, willpower, and motivation.

Whitten stresses the significance of experimentation and individualization throughout the book. He advises readers to keep track of their progress and make adjustments based on their particular requirements and objectives.

In general, "Smarter Not Harder" is a comprehensive biohacking guide for people who want to improve their mental and physical performance. The book is supported by scientific research and offers readers useful strategies and advice that they can put into practice in their own lives.

The book is separated into four fundamental segments, each tending to an alternate part of biohacking. The primary area investigates the standards of biohacking, including sustenance, rest, and exercise. The author explains how to make these aspects of life work best so that you can perform at your best.

The author offers strategies for enhancing memory, concentration, and creativity in order to maximize brain function. The author discusses supplements, nootropics, and other methods for improving cognitive function.

Techniques for improving physical performance, such as strength training, endurance training, and recovery, are discussed in the third section. The author explains how to monitor and enhance physical performance by utilizing technology like biofeedback and wearable devices.

In general, the book's final section covers advanced biohacking methods like hormone optimization, genetic testing, and strategies to fight aging. The author discusses cutting-edge methods and technologies for enhancing well-being and health.

Asprey further stresses the significance of self-experimentation and self-awareness throughout the entire book. He encourages readers to monitor their progress and modify their biohacking strategies in accordance with their particular requirements and objectives.

Fitness and exercise are the focus of the book's third section. High-intensity interval training (HIIT) and resistance training are two of the training methods Greenfield discusses, as are strategies for maximizing recovery and avoiding injury.

Recovery and sleep are the subjects of the fourth chapter of the book. Greenfield investigates a variety of methods for enhancing the quality of sleep, such as enhancing the sleep environment and making use of supplements and technology. Additionally, he talks about how recovery affects physical and mental performance.

The book also focuses on longevity and prevention of aging. Asprey investigates different techniques for broadening life expectancy and advancing healthspan, for example, diminishing aggravation, enhancing chemical levels, and utilizing enhancements and innovation to work on cell capability.

Throughout the book, Asprey offers readers who want to begin biohacking their own health and performance helpful pointers and suggestions that can be put into action. In addition, he provides personal anecdotes and case studies to demonstrate the usefulness of various biohacking strategies.

Overall, "Smarter Not Harder" is a comprehensive biohacking guide that gives readers the knowledge and tools they need to improve their health and well-being, extend their lifespan, and optimize their physical and mental performance.

The author interrogates the biological and psychological factors that contribute to food addiction in the first section. For instance, eating foods high in sugar and fat causes the brain to release dopamine. She also talks about how important it is to identify and address emotional eating patterns.

I get the impression from a lot of this book that Dave has run out of money and thought he could put his previous ideas into a new book. Most people won't be able to afford many of the hacks. This appears to be additional advertising material for his investments and businesses. You can get more worth doing a lot of this examination yourself on youtube.

If you've never read one of his books, pick it up. Have you ever been to a movie and come out with your imagination so piqued that it gave you so much energy and motivation to keep going? This book accomplishes tenfold that. I had to force myself to stop listening to this non-fiction book because I was more excited about its content than any good fiction. Although I have only listened to a few chapters, I have found that "Smarter Not Harder" contains so much useful information that I frequently hit rewind to ensure that I have fully comprehended what is being taught. If you haven't already read Dave's books and adhered to his teachings, you won't be able to find most of this information elsewhere, or at least not all of it.

Dave Asprey shares the results of his years of unrelenting self-teaching and experimentation with the world rather than keeping this priceless knowledge and these "secrets" to himself and his circle or selling them only to wealthy customers. It is a present. You will get more out of this book than you can imagine if you read it or listen to it, as well as all of Dave's books. Dave, thank you for showing people how to understand that they can take charge of their health and improve their lives infinitely. I am very happy and appreciative of your knowledge, which assisted me in losing a lot of weight, lifting me out of deep sorrow, and regaining much of my mental and physical health, which I had unintentionally damaged greatly.

What a treasure trove of life-enhancing information and strategies!

Dave is an amazing writer who is great at gathering new information and then breaking it down into digestible chunks.

This book is filled to the brim with genius gems, providing such concentrated and simple health shortcuts. It has the impression of exploding into the world like a treasure trove of secrets.

I know I could give this book to my 77-year-old parents and know that they would be able to understand the information and be inspired to improve their lives with little effort because it is so accessible and supported by credible, data-proven science.

I've never seen so much revolutionary new information in one place as in this book. Additionally, he weaves science and spirituality in such a unique and expansive way! It's powerful stuff!

I'm into biohacking, health, and fitness, and trying to keep up with all the healthy activities I should be doing to keep my mind and body strong can feel like a second job.

This book was truly useful in telling me the best way to utilize my time all the more really with the things I'm doing to ensure I'm enhancing for results. Take exercise as an example. I probably won't waste my time going on another run when there are now so many other options that are better for my body, more effective, and help me achieve the results I want.

One more incredible asset from Asprey. I find it useful to have a concise source of the information I have learned organized into a single book for easy reference as an entrepreneur with a busy schedule. Dave always does a great job of making tried-and-true hacks that many of us in the health and wellness industry use available to the public.

based on research and personal experience, this book is well-written and simple to follow. An excellent purchase for everyone. Get this book if you only want to find what truly works and not want to delve deeply. Incredible work Dave!

I believe that everyone desires more TIME. Time to enjoy with family, time to finish work and time to exercise and fill your own cup with much required confidence. Everything from fitness to nutrition to spiritual and mindfulness practices is covered in this book. Anything goes. You will learn how to complete it more effectively in the book. Wonderful read! Already making adjustments to my peloton classes to adhere to REHIT: D. Many thanks, Dave!

a lot of mixed feelings regarding this. Although there is new information and excellent advice, I am uncertain of its long-term viability. The diet is extremely strict. Certain kinds of fish, grass-fed beef, butter, dairy, and a small number of vegetables are the "good foods." Then, it goes into great detail about a lot of supplements that can take the place of food.

He also provides valuable advice on natural spices and herbs.

Having said that, a few days after eliminating some of the vegetables he suggested, my 15-year-old hand dermatitis significantly improved. I'm giving you all the stars in the world for that alone.

He definitely has the right idea, but a lot of the advice seems too crazy to me. But that's the point: you have to do things that normal people don't do in order to feel better.

I'm going to keep trying at least some of the hacks to see how they work out.

Made in United States
North Haven, CT
03 April 2023

34987394R00015